ICONS OF THE INVISIBLE GOD

selected sculptures of Peter Eugene Ball

in cathedrals, churches, chapels

and private collections

CHEVRON

To Vera and Lawson

Edited by Elaine Kazimierczuk

Designed by Terry Miller Associates   0115 9240814

First published in Great Britain by Chevron Books 1999

CHEVRON

Chevron Books
PO Box 5723
Bilsthorpe
NEWARK
Notts
NG22 8TF

ISBN No: 0 9535627 0 0

British Library CIP Data - a catalogue record for this book is available from the British Library.

All dimensions refer to height x width x depth where appropriate.

Printed by Wayzgoose

"Christ is the icon of the invisible God;
all things were created through him and for him;"

liturgical phrase taken from The Book of Occasional Services,
based on the text: Colossians, chapter 1 verse 15

CONTENTS

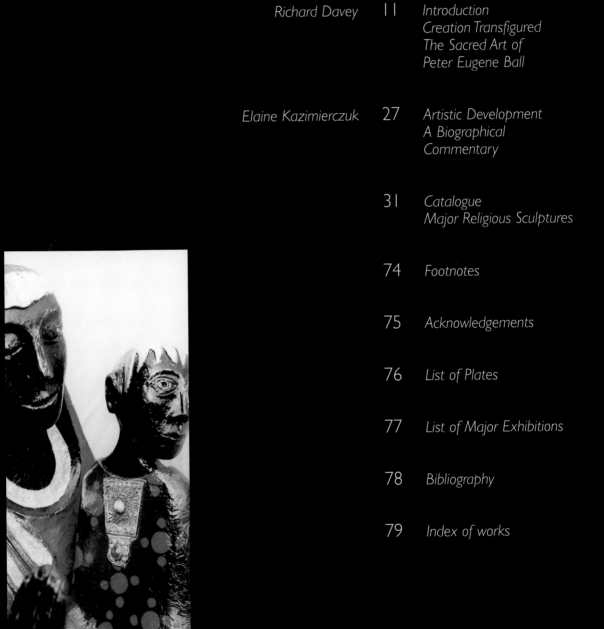

The Christian Church in this country has been ambivalent about images, especially three dimensional ones, since the Reformation. The most extreme Reformers can be recognised by their condemnation of the visual aids to devotion and their wreckage of them. But ever since the Oxford Movement rediscovered the quickening of the spirit that can be sparked by ancient liturgies and icons, sculpted figures have begun to find their way back into the empty spaces once occupied by their gracious Medieval predecessors. In the nineteenth century the replacement sculptures tended to be rather tame imitations of the past, seldom showing the fire of contemporary paintings by the Pre-Raphaelites, or even the intensity of Burne-Jones windows. In the twentieth century a few intrepid ecclesiastical patrons have sought to enlist the contribution of artists who were in full flight over secular fields. Some few - Epstein and Eric Gill for instance, the earlier Henry Moore at Northampton, and more recently perhaps Elizabeth Frink, - have proved to be swallows able to nest around the altar. But none has matched the remarkable, and to begin with, improbable, aptitude of Peter Ball to conceive sculptures which not only settle without conflict into ancient and sacred spaces, but look, from the day of arrival, as if they had always been there. How has it happened?

The Eucharistic Church, whether Roman, Orthodox or relatively High Anglican, has agreed that Images may not be worshipped, but they may be venerated. All over Europe there survive cult statues of great age, of venerability, before which veneration is the natural response. It is more difficult to offer veneration before a carving which is evidently new. Let us take an obvious example. Westminster Cathedral possesses two statues of Our Lady of Westminster[1]. One of wood, was subsequently adorned with two crowns, one for daily use (now it would appear stolen) and another for Feast Days (apparently sold in the 1960's by Cardinal Heenan for the relief of the poor). These crowns were both designed by Omar Ramsden, no less. The figure was of the best workmanship in what we might term the Burnes & Oates tradition at its heyday in c1920. It now stands in the Sacristy. The other is a fifteenth century alabaster, one of the eleven surviving relatively large seated English high reliefs of the subject. It is this which holds the place of honour, at the entrance to the Lady Chapel, and before it ranks of candles ever burn. To many observers the gentle and comely wooden figure might seem more immediately attractive; but for all its over-large Virgin's head and mannequin-like Christ Child, the very remoteness, the antiquity, of the alabaster excites - veneration.

In his youth Peter Ball made several witty sculptures which combined pieces of drift-wood and unlikely flotsam into quixotic and endearing conjunctions. It was a vein of creativity going back perhaps, to Picasso's famous bicycle seat and handlebars, and of course to Henry Moore and Barbara Hepworth's seaside pebbles. But when Peter Ball started incorporating drift-wood and apparently second-hand metal-work into his religious commissions, something new happened. The weathered and twisted nature of his woods, the varied and distressed patinas of his metal components, contributed to his figures the dimension of age.

Peter Ball never copies, in the literal sense, a Romanesque hanging Christus. The elements of his work are probably a combination of roots tormented among rocks, and tree trunks many times re-used in ships and Tudor houses, brought together with hand-beaten copper and brass plates which serve both as physical links, and as memories of Mosan gilding and enamelling. So his Christus has, in the nature of its composition, the battle-scarred endurance of a time-worn Romanesque Christus.

The large eyed narrow bearded heads of Romanesque art come naturally to Peter Ball. He is not the heir of the comely Gothic but of the tormented prophets of Souillac, or even further back, of Celtic spirit figures. His way of seeing is most suited, perhaps, to commissions for the Hanging Rood, or for a gaunt Pietà, but there is a tenderness in his treatment of the Nativity, and in his Madonnas he can suggest something of the mystery that hedges about, for instance, the Holy Virgin of Rocamadour. But this sculptor is in no way a pasticheur of the Age of Faith. He has none of the subservience that would imply. His visual quotations are made with panache.

My father taught me to observe the difference between amateur musicians and professionals. The amateurs talked about music all the time, and with bated breath. The professionals preferred to talk among friends about something else, and if they were drawn into the music field, tended to keep to the nuts and bolts of it. Peter Ball is, in my father's terms, a thorough professional. You may be able to persuade him to tell you how a particular carving came together - and like a Baroque jeweller taking his theme from a distorted pearl, he listens to the configuration of the battered shape he has to hand - but you wont get him to talk about inspiration. Nevertheless a significant number of churches and cathedrals have turned to him lately for that focus of prayer torn from them in the 1530's. You will find his work also in private chapels and Monastic Houses: anywhere the life of the spirit really matters. The proof of inspiration appears to be in the achievement.

If Peter Ball, the most cheerfully down-to-earth of men, is at all mystified by the way his career has developed, he would do well to remember that God has a sense of humour.

Pamela Lady Wedgewood, Lewes

March 1999

Creation Transfigured
The Sacred Art of Peter Eugene Ball

SHIP OF FOOLS
95 x 110cm PRIVATE COLLECTION

SHIP OF FOOLS *detail*

full size 95 x 110cm PRIVATE COLLECTION

Works of art have always reflected and helped to define the society out of which they are formed. In the Middle Ages western art was an expression of the cohesive vision of Christendom; whilst the 'history' paintings, landscapes and portraits of the Renaissance and Age of Enlightenment celebrated the glory of the human spirit. But at the end of the Twentieth Century western society is no longer bound together by a common vision and purpose. It has become a culture of extremes and contradictions that celebrates both the ordinary and the mysterious, despair and hope. Yet it is rare for artists to reflect the disparate nature of contemporary culture in their work. Instead they prefer to concentrate on just one aspect of it. The idiosyncratic work of Peter Eugene Ball, however, stands out; for its very structure is a celebration and expression of this diversity. He reflects the concerns of artists such as Richard Wentworth and Jean Dubuffet in his use of ordinary and discarded objects as the inspiration and materials for his sculptures. But he covers them with beaten metal and gold leaf and transforms them into images taken from mythology and Christian iconography. The result has been timeless images that capture the mystical realism of our age.

Ball's forms and materials reflect the love of medieval religious art that has informed his work since he was introduced to Romanesque sculpture as a student in the late 1950's. Here he found works of art that were not jewel-like and precious, but gritty and down to earth. They were created by unknown individuals who, like modern graffiti artists, covered any available material and surface with their colourful and vivid imagery. Ball is attracted to the anonymity and immediacy of these images because they echo his own artistic aims to create works of art that are not overshadowed by any artistic cultism. He finds this same quality in the work of Jean Dubuffet. In the 1940's Dubuffet had sought to create objects that would appeal more to the man in the street than to a mere handful of specialists. By stripping away the layers of acquired culture he wanted to discover an earlier state of childlike innocence and amazement.[2] The result was a series of assemblages, made in the 1950's, that were created from a wide range of everyday materials and detritus, including fragments of burnt out cars, grapevines, trees and tobacco. In 1959, Dubuffet produced a number of sculptures from driftwood that have clearly influenced Ball's own work. In the gnarled and contorted forms of Dubuffet's 'The Old Man of the Beach' we find an echo of the twisting and writhing forms of **Sea Creature,** 1996 (private collection). But whilst Dubuffet leaves the natural form largely untouched, Ball draws out the image he perceives within the wood, and transforms the natural material with the addition of one of his characteristic heads.

Ball's fascination with everyday ordinary materials can be seen in his earliest sculptures, which were made of plastic. But whilst these works were made from modern materials, their inspiration came from Romanesque models. For Ball, however, the technical process was too time consuming.[3] Like Dubuffet, he found his inspiration in objects that had been discarded and washed up - pieces of driftwood, railway sleepers, ropes and bells. These objects not only provide the materials but also the stimulus for his sculpture. He approaches each piece of wood with an open mind, allowing the natural forms to dictate the subject that will emerge. Many of the objects that he finds are left largely untouched. The body of the **Standing Virgin,** 1995 (private collection) is still clearly a sea-worn, eroded plank, whose sinuous outline is reminiscent of the swaying form of medieval Virgins. It is only through the addition of a diminutive head formed from beaten copper, and two hanging objects, that we are aware of Ball's

SEA CREATURE

95 x 46cm PRIVATE COLLECTION

intervention. The burnished surface of the head itself blends into the weathered tones of the wood, so that it appears to be an integral part of the natural object. Other figures, however, are built up from a number of elements. These works can change radically during the process of creation, as each individual element suggests a specific interpretation. A Tower of Babel can turn into a Virgin, as the addition of different elements suggests a more appropriate response to the materials. The process of combining disparate elements into a single image is one that fascinates Ball. He is able to transform the function and meaning of ordinary objects by placing them onto the basic form of a Madonna, or other religious figure. These 'mechanical' sculptures are a playful and humorous attempt to use an abstract vocabulary in the creation of a figurative image. In **Mechanical Virgin,** 1995 (private collection), the addition of a woman's head onto a tower constructed from elements including a wooden ball, a cup, a scallop shell and a small metal crown transfigures an abstract jumble into an elaborate image of the Virgin. It becomes a surreal still life, in which each of the objects contributes to a wider understanding of the whole to reveal the qualities of the Madonna, rather than her portrait. These mechanical virgins have a timeless quality that combines the abstract and surreal qualities of modern art with the primitive character of a votive image. Through them Ball explores the complex interplay between the sacred and secular that allows an ordinary object to reveal something of God. A constant source of inspiration for Ball is driftwood, which he collects mainly from one specific beach on the Sussex coast. The prolonged action of sea and elements transforms predictable appearance of wood into something that has a rich and varied texture, shape and colour. Over time the geometric form of a plank can come to resemble the windswept and eroded features of a weather beaten medieval sculpture. And then, as the raw material of the artist, it can be made into a work of art. This is another example of the complex process of metamorphosis and transformation that so fascinates Ball, by which one object can take on the qualities of another. There is a rich irony in the process that allows a piece of wood that was originally part of a ship to become the material from which an artist can then create his image of a ship.

Once Ball has chosen his materials, the subject and forms of the finished work emerge naturally out of the process of creation. Although the choice of subject matter is left completely open, in reality Ball has returned to a limited number of themes throughout his career. Images of the Ship of Fools, harpies, pilgrims, angels, Christ and the Virgin, reflect his interest in Greek and Roman mythology, angels, demons, Celtic gods, and Christian Churches. Religious imagery has fascinated Ball since he first encountered it as a child on the walls of churches. Although he himself is not a Christian, the influence of Christ on history and society is something that he cannot avoid. In the sublime beauty and otherworldliness of religious images such as Matthias Grunewald's Isenheim Altarpiece, Ball finds a sense of transcendence and hope that he does not experience elsewhere. And it is in his own act of creativity that Ball has discovered a language to describe God and his yearning for the divine. His work represents the journey into the unknown that is so eloquently captured by his image of the **Ship of Fools,** 1998 (private collection). His subjects may have particular historical and religious associations, but Ball sees a wider relevance in them. They address not only the specific dogmas of Christianity, but also the wider issues of where we come from, and what our purpose in life is. A sculpture of the Virgin is both an image of the Mother of Christ, and also one of fecundity and womanhood. With bells and prayer stones hanging by their sides Ball's Virgins become pagan priestesses, goddesses, and images of Mother Earth. They are representations of a mother and child, rather

MECHANICAL VIRGIN

94 x 37 x 28cm PRIVATE COLLECTION

than the more specific Madonna and Christ Child. The same ambiguities are found in the figure of Christ which is both a symbol of Everyman and the portrayal of an actual human being; a real man who has both suffered pain and transcended it. In one image we can find portrayed both death and resurrection, hope and despair. But if the Virgin can portray a goddess, and Christ can be Everyman, it is also possible to see in the sculptures of Zeus, the fool, and in a pilgrim, the image of Christ.

Ball not only found a rich source of subject matter in Romanesque art, but also an expressive language that has had a profound effect on his work. His early images of the crucifixion have a crudity and monumentality that is clearly related to the strong,

THE ARTIST'S STUDIO

emotional forms of Romanesque sculpture. In his *Crucifixion,* 1984, (Birmingham Cathedral) the body of Christ is stylized and formal. The legs and arms are graphic gestures that bear little resemblance to human anatomy, whilst the torso blends seamlessly and impossibly into an elaborate loincloth. It is only in the face of Christ that we encounter a sense of human suffering and pain. Despite his idealised and simplified features, this is clearly the portrait of a real person. The silhouette and lines of Ball's images help to clarify the subject matter and establish its emotional quality. Whilst the face may portray pain, the body resembles the muscled torso of a Hercules. The unbending linear outline of the body that follows the strong vertical and horizontal forms of the cross suggests triumph, not death. Gradually, however, the monumental outlines of these early works have softened and become more sinuous. Through his use of driftwood, with its natural shapes and curvilinear forms, he has produced works that are closer to the elongated and exaggerated forms of the thirteenth century than those of the Romanesque. The gentle curve that articulates the right hand edge of his *Driftwood Crucifix,* 1994 (private collection) provides an emotional counter to the broken stump that serves as its left arm. The face of Christ may be drawn in pain, but the curved form of the figure extends upwards into a single hand that reaches towards heaven and Resurrection.

Although Ball has often used Christian imagery in his work, it is only since the early 1980's that this previously private imagery has become known to a wider audience. Ball's figures of Christ and the Virgin have been commissioned by churches and cathedrals throughout the country, where they are now seen within the architecture that inspired their forms. Their gentle curves and muted tones blend perfectly into their surroundings. The majority of these works have a formality and elaborate decoration that is far removed from the spontaneous and simple quality of the driftwood and mechanical works. Instead, there is a quiet dignity in his seated figures of the Mother and Child that is reminiscent of medieval reliquaries and devotional objects.

DRIFTWOOD CRUCIFIX

65 x 58cm PRIVATE COLLECTION

The application of beaten metal and gold leaf to the wood contributes to their sense of sublimity and richness. Whilst his driftwood sculptures rely upon the natural form of the wood to provide the outline and create a sense of emotional intensity, the majority of the church commissions are built up pieces in which he has had to create the outline himself. In *Our Lady of Lambley,* 1991 (Parish Church of the Holy and Undivided Trinity), he has formed the outstretched arms of the Christ Child into an expressive curve that suggests welcome and acceptance. This is reinforced by the gentle line of the Virgin's neck as she looks down at her son. But Ball's use of line is not confined to the outline of his figures. Across the surface of his work he gouges lines into the wood and leaves trails of rivets in the metal. These both animate the surface and break down the natural rigidity of the outline. A further sense of depth and animation is to be found in *Silver Madonna,* 1996 (private collection) where lines of small copper rivets cut across the direction of the incised lines. These swirls and spirals create a sense of energy and movement that echoes the sketch-like, fluid quality of the driftwood forms. The same sense of surface animation is to be found in Ball's figures of Christ.

SILVER MADONNA

105 x 40cm PRIVATE COLLECTION

SMALL CHRIST IN MAJESTY

c. 48 x 56cm PRIVATE COLLECTION

BLACK VIRGIN

c. 95 x 35cm PRIVATE COLLECTION

Throughout his career he has returned to the image of Christ, portraying him as the figure of a boy sitting on his mother's knee, the condemned man of the Ecce Homo, and the dead body of the Pieta.

But the majority of Church commissions represent the robed figure of the Christ in Majesty. The long robes that these figures are wearing are reminiscent of Romanesque crucifixes from Catalonia, or the 'Holy Face' of Lucca, which was said to have been carved by Nicodemus.[4] His arms are still outstretched, but he is separated from the cross itself. In the strong outline of the cruciform shape, which is broken only slightly by the suggestive form of a curve, there is revealed the image of a Christ who has triumphed over suffering and death. In many of Ball's robed Christs he covers the surfaces with a network of dynamic lines that are not only decorative but also enhance and define the emotional and narrative content of the work. In *Small Christ in Majesty,* 1981 (private collection) the lower part of the robe is energized by a sinuous line that emerges out of four converging lines and ends in a shepherd's hook. Along the lower edge of the arms the stylized form of a bird is suggested by a gently curving line. Its shape echoes that of the dove which comes to reveal the divinity of Christ in Piero della Francesca's painting of the Baptism. These swirling lines and concentric circles, which evoke the spirals and marks found on Neolithic stones as well as the clinging 'damp-fold' drapery forms of Romanesque art, give the work a sense of antiquity and mystery. Not all the forms are curvilinear, however. The wood and metal surfaces of the **Christus Rex,** 1987 (Southwell Minster) and the **Christus,** 1995 (Monmouth School Chapel) are decorated with diagonal lines and chevrons that resemble the abstract patterns carved into the nave pillars of Durham Cathedral and other Norman and Romanesque buildings. The regularity of these patterns acts like camouflage to dissolve the solidity of the figure.

Ball's use of colour further contributes to the subtle energy of these works. The layer of beaten metals that covers the wood is transformed through the application of heat, varnish and oxidants into a myriad of iridescent tones and colours. The surface shimmers like an abstract painting to excite the eye with the hint of intricate depths and nuances. The swirling lines that animate the surface of **Crucifix,** 1992, (St Mary's, Nottingham) terminate in roundels of beaten metal which resemble a peacock's feather. Their dark copper centres seem to pierce the golden haloes that surround them to expose the hidden interior of the work. The same effect can be seen in the driftwood sculptures. In **Driftwood Virgin,** 1991, (private collection) the polished surface of the beaten metal patches resonates with the matt surface of the wood to create a powerful dialogue between surface and depth, light and dark. At times Ball punctuates the polished metal surfaces with streaks and splashes of verdigris. The rich green serves to animate the surface as well as giving the work a sense of antiquity. Occasionally he will paint the

religious sculptures. This more obvious application of colour, which is governed by the use of appropriate liturgical colours, results in works that have an alien, and mystical appearance. In *Black Virgin*, 1990 (private collection) the circular red patterns that cover the figures of the Mother and Child not only animate the surface but also serve to emphasise the bond between them. Their black features are offset however, by gold leaf, which has been used to define the flame-like arrows of hair that point towards the face of Christ, and also to encircle the head of the Virgin. The burnished gold stands out against the dark surface to highlight and stress the important aspects of the image. Gold leaf provides Ball with a versatile material that offers a wealth of artistic possibilities. Like paint, it can produce gestural marks that are richly varied and expressive. On the body of the *Small Christ in Majesty* it creates nebulous cloud-like forms that seem to hover above the surface of the sculpture. And in *Driftwood Crucifix,* the gilded face of Christ seems to radiate light, so that a vision of his divinity and glory shine out of the transfigured features.

Ball's sculptures are defined by their remarkable faces. Their presence can transform even the simplest piece of driftwood into the image of an angel, or Zeus. The strong curve of the elongated sphere which forms the head is echoed in the curves which articulate the features of the face. The gentle curves of the eyebrows, eyes, nose, and mouth generate a sense of serenity and rest in the figure. Ball contributes to this emotional intensity by giving many of his figures closed eyes. This is not intended to suggest sleep, but rather a moment of sublime contemplation and concentration. But the closed eyes also create a sense of separation and distance between the image and the viewer, inviting contemplation rather than direct involvement. It is therefore significant when figures are given open eyes. Their wide-eyed stares confront the viewer with a direct gaze that is both challenging and compassionate. These are clearly not abstract, imaginary faces but portraits of individuals; each with a different story to tell.

Colour and line are an essential element of Ball's paintings as well as his sculpture. His paintings have a vitality and spontaneity which echoes the freedom of the simplest driftwood sculptures. But whereas the form and subject of these sculptures comes from the wood itself, the paintings are reliant upon the imagination of the artist alone. Although they appear to be sketches for sculptures, they are conceived as works in their own right. They are the translation from one media into another of recurrent themes and forms. In the paintings the strong silhouette that defines the sculptural forms is shattered by bold and dynamic brushstrokes. The surface of the paper seems to explode with energy and life as paint is dragged vigorously across it, whilst the dribbles and splashes of paint echo those of Jackson Pollock.

MADONNA AND CHILD

102 x 32cm PRIVATE COLLECTION

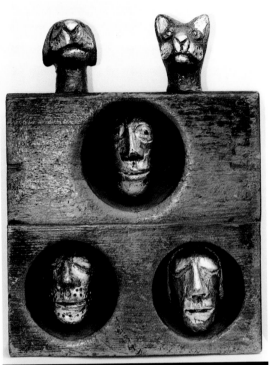

The paintings capture the feeling of hope and joy that is so evident in the sculptures. This is reinforced by Ball's use of gold paint which stands out with a luminous brilliance against the flat appearance of the other colours. The dynamic relationship between colours creates complex layers of depth and space that suggest both an interior dimension and a world beyond.

The same luminosity can be found in a series of crude paintings that Ball made in the early 1980's. In them he painted mermaids and mythical beasts; the hybrid forms of medieval grotesques. These primitive paintings resemble both the graffiti images of Dubuffet, and also the most archaic and simple forms of Romanesque sculpture. Even the paint has been mixed with sand to give a rough texture that resembles stone. In many of them the figures stand within an architectural arcade that suggests the west front of a medieval cathedral. The figures and disembodied heads which emerge from the dark archways are like Ball's sculpture, *Companionship,* 1979 (private collection). In this, and similar images, he placed a series of heads in the hollows of a block of wood to explore ideas of both isolation and friendship. In *Niche Figure* 1981, (artist's collection) the figure that stands within the niche has been created from a stack of basic geometric shapes which offer only the merest suggestion of the human form. It resembles one of the 'mechanical virgins' as it combines disparate elements to create the image of a body. The subject of these works is not explicitly religious.

Although the forms may resemble medieval religious art, they are not identified as saints or biblical figures. But as with many of Ball's non-religious images, it is in his use of line and colour, rather than the subject matter, that the sacred dimension of the work is revealed. The figures have a luminosity that is ethereal and mysterious. Like the first light, they seem to emerge out of a dark, empty void.

For forty years Ball has used the discarded objects of society to produce artworks of intense beauty and mystery. Although the objects he has created are in one sense nothing more than simple sculptures and paintings, they have consistently revealed their potential to be something far more. Through his transformation of the contours and evocative forms of driftwood and junk he has exposed images of the Virgin, Christ, and mythological subjects which have a timeless and sacred quality. And through the use of iridescent colours, sinuous patterns and intriguing textures he has changed the strong outlines and formal limitations of his church commissions into images of promise and hope that reveal the mystical potential of creation. Once we have glimpsed the world through Ball's eyes we can never see things in the same way again. For mysteries have been exposed, creation transformed, and the presence of God revealed.

Richard Davey
Bury St Edmunds
February 1999

A Biographical Commentary

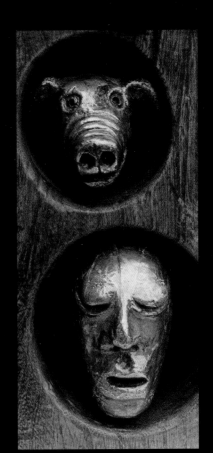

Peter Eugene Ball was born in Coventry, Warwickshire in 1943. He attended Coventry College of Art from 1957 until 1962. He joined the Majorie Parr Gallery, King's Road, Chelsea in 1961, where he had his first one-man show in 1967. Since then he has devoted himself to his work, exhibiting and selling through galleries in America and across Europe.

From an early age, the powerful visual images of paintings, sculptures, and architectural forms have made a deep impression on Peter Ball. His interest in art and architecture was aroused whilst he was still at secondary school, where enlightened history teachers brought their subject alive by taking the boys on frequent outings. One of the earliest of these was to Southwell Minster, Nottinghamshire, which many years later, by coincidence became the first cathedral where a major work was commissioned. Peter Ball acquired much first-hand knowledge, whilst accompanying Geoffrey Saunders, an art history tutor, on trips around the British Isles, during the 1960's. Together they made a photographic survey of ancient buildings and monuments throughout England, Scotland and Wales. From this Peter Ball developed in particular, a feeling for Celtic and Romanesque carvings both religious and secular.

Peter still spends what time he can visiting the places which are a constant source of fascination to him - rural churches, grand cathedrals and other ancient monuments where he is all the time absorbing his surroundings, sifting their very atmosphere for "visual quotations" which he later incorporates into his own work. This ability to comprehend and interpret visual messages has enabled him to become part of a

stream of creative activity evident in the sculptors and masons of early Christian monuments and their pagan forebears.

His unconscious sense of the "genius loci" enables Peter Ball to know intuitively, for instance, when he visits a place prior to creating a design for a commission, how a sculpture will need to turn out. In his book "Images or Idols?" Keith Walker refers to the commissioning of the Pietà for the Lady Chapel of Winchester Cathedral - *"...he seemed to look into the Chapel for a brief moment and took no measurements.... In imagination he could see almost immediately the sculpture in its context. When it was unveiled we found that the colours matched those of the surrounding stained glass, painted walls and altar and that its vertical linear form blended well with the perpendicular architecture of the Chapel"*.

In his constant pursuit of suitable stuff to undergo the metamorphosis into one of his saints or satyrs, Peter Ball haunts sea-shores, flea-markets, junk-shops - anywhere that might yield a good crop of "objets trouvés". One object may reveal its potential straight away, whilst another unlikely looking thing will be taken home, and sit gathering dust at the back of the studio for years, until suddenly he recognises how to incorporate it into a piece of sculpture and all at once the object looks as if it had been made for that purpose.

Peter Ball has two sons by his first marriage in 1963 and a daughter and a son from his second marriage in 1982. He now lives and works in Nottinghamshire, with part of the year being spent in France, at his farmhouse in the Loire Valley, a starting point for exploring the rest of Europe. Not only is there the remarkable architecture of grand cathedrals such as Chartres, but also that of tiny ancient churches such as those on the Pilgrimage route to Santiago di Compostella, a journey which he made himself in 1982. Peter Ball enjoys these humble buildings, which as his friend and author of many well-known topographical books Henry Thorold likes to say, are in their own right "Testaments to the Almighty" (even when they are declared "redundant", as with some abandoned church out in the remote Linconshire Fens). But more than that, many of these places are also treasure houses, crammed with images and icons where Peter Ball taps into an artistic tradition stretching back centuries. Sculptures such as the Black Virgin in St Mary's Cathedral, Krakow, dripping with votive offerings, which radiate an extraordinary beauty in the glow of flickering candle flames. These objects seem to exude mystery as if visibly covered with a patina of prayer formed over centuries of devotion.

Whilst most of Peter Ball's work does not have an overtly religious theme, he has drawn in these influences, distilling them into the recurrent themes apparent in his unique work. In an age which often seems on the surface to be increasingly crass and godless, many people find themselves at a loss to articulate their emotions about art and even more so when those feelings take on a spiritual dimension. Somehow the work of Peter Ball gets through, dispensing with this deficiency, and providing a medium for the expression of our thoughts and prayers.

Elaine Kazimierczuk 1999

Major Religious Sculptures

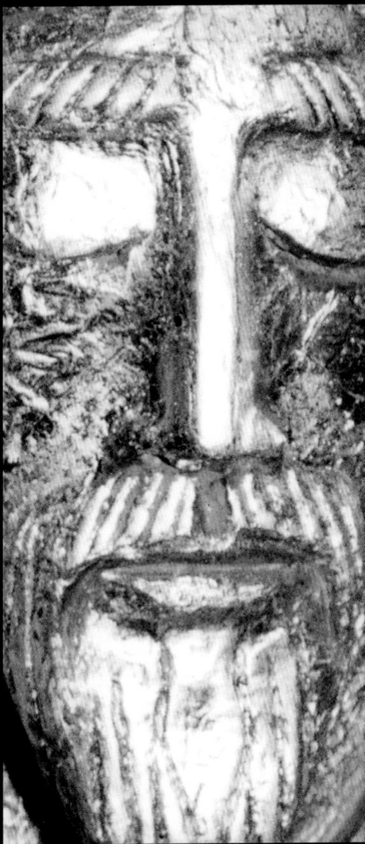

RISTUS

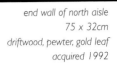

end wall of north aisle
75 x 32cm
driftwood, pewter, gold leaf
acquired 1992

Peter Ball's simple figure of St John the Baptist fits particularly well within this remarkable little church, with its fascinating remnants of medieval wall paintings. The sculpture is made of driftwood, partly covered in pewter, making a highly textured surface like the rough garment of a hermit. The figure stands slightly hesitant, wide-eyed and with an innocent saintly air. His left hand is extended as if to invite friendship; with his right hand he seems to be making a gesture of his sincerity. The sculpture was dedicated by the Bishop of Warwick during a memorial service to David Ball, in 1992.

This work was donated by Peter Ball in memory of his grandmother, Elizabeth Print, who died in 1951 aged 65, and also to his younger brother David Ball, who died in 1989, at the age of 44.

The Ball children used to spend their summer holidays at their grandmother's cottage in Baginton.

above pulpit
60 x 40cm
wood, brass, gold leaf
acquired 1992

One of the artist's smallest commissions, this image of the risen Christ, in bright gold against a simple red cross, has a fresh lustre that contrasts well with the dark polished oak of the carved fifteenth century pews and pulpit. The Christ has a somewhat naive

appearance. His childlike features are similar to those primitive images seen on early Romanesque carvings; an excellent example of this type of work can be found nearby on the stone font at All Saints' Church, West Markham in Nottinghamshire.

The sculpture was commissioned and donated by Canon Charles Young, vicar of St Giles for 17 years, to mark his retirement.

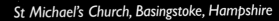
above chancel arch
244 x 183cm
wood, copper, gold leaf
acquired 1997

This majestic figure of Christ is a powerful yet graceful image, the richness of the copper and gold contrasting strongly with the cold grey stone against which it is set, bringing warmth and light into the church.

The commission was funded by grants from: The Jerusalem Trust (a charity founded by the Sainsbury family), Hampshire County Council, Basingstoke and Deane Borough Council, Foundation for Sport and the Arts, and a donation in memory of John Williams.

This is an image of Christ in Glory-

..." a High Priest of the Eternal Sacrifice, ... an eloquent point of focus in this splendid but austere church".

from a commendation of the work by Pamela Wedgewood.

33

north aisle chapel;
crucifix - 148 x 144cm
wood, copper, gold leaf
acquired 1984
figures - c.110 x 20 cm
wood, pewter, brass
acquired 1986

The contemplative mood of this sculpture shows Christ as a victim. This stylised crucifix creates a strong and compelling image. Here is Christ the Man, and although the anatomical detail is stylised and restrained, yet there is a visible tension in the stiffened body tortured by pain. The angle of the head and feet express human suffering and sorrow. The style is similar to that of Medieval crucifixes, and brings to mind such works as the Gabel Crucifix (1304), in the Church of St Maria im Kapitol in Cologne. Though centuries apart, the crucifixes stir the same intense emotions.

The work was originally exhibited at the Bleddfa Festival in 1983. The Very Reverend Basil Moss, Provost at that time, saw the Crucifix whilst on holiday with his wife in the Welsh Borders and was struck by its power.

The Crucifix acquired in 1984, was joined in 1986 by the addition of St Mary and St John in the form of candle holders which stand on the altar table in front

of the crucifix. These two figures, together with the Crucifix, complete the Calvary, and with their faces turned away from the cross, they express their despair and pity.

The works were donated by the Friends of Birmingham Cathedral.

not yet in permanent location
104 x 28 x 25cm
wood, pewter, copper, gold leaf
acquired 1997

Originally, the church had approached Peter Ball with a view to commissioning a small statue to occupy a niche over the porch on the exterior of the church. In order to show the fabric committee the exact nature of the materials with which he worked, Peter Ball took along the Madonna and Child to a meeting. Once the sculpture was placed inside the church, it was a unanimous decision not to let it out again. As a result, the commissioning group set about rapidly raising the necessary funds, and so the church acquired the piece.

Such a magnificent church deserves such a beautiful sculpture. Sunlight streams in from the clear windows filling the building with a pure light so that the golden faces of Mary and Jesus appear to be radiant. On Mary's right wrist hang two small objects like devotional gifts - symbols of faith - a bell and a little wooden case containing an Islamic prayer for safe-keeping. Jesus has a distant look as if in the knowledge of what is to come. Mary's expression seems to suggest that she is listening to her own inner foreboding thoughts, whilst she opens her hands to offer up her child to the world.

foyer, Hope Centre
122 x 190 x 30cm
wood, copper, gold leaf
acquired 1997

An unusual format, this work depicts an image of Christ bringing a message of hope to those who come to him, standing, arms outstretched in a warm and compassionate gesture inviting the onlooker to draw nearer. Jesus is shown preaching to three disciples crouching in rapt attention at his feet.

The community and parish commissioned the work as a memorial to Ros Harding.

above chancel arch
122 x 76cm
wood, copper, gold leaf
acquired 1996

This quiet and contemplative image of Christ crucified hangs gracefully over the chancel arch of this charming village church set in an idyllic patch of rural Hampshire. The elongated form of Christ's body, conveying suffering and sublimity, and the crude styling of the cross, suggesting rough carpentry, fit well with the simple forms of the early Norman architecture.

The church is thankfully kept unlocked and is a little haven for solitude and meditation.

The work was donated by the Friends of St Andrew's, Chilcomb.

above chancel arch
280 x 250cm
wood, copper, gold leaf
acquired 1998

After arson caused massive fire damage to All Saint's in 1996, a small group of parishioners were determined that as part of the restoration, they should have a work referring to the church's resurrection from its ashes; and so the plan to commission an image of a Risen Christ was conceived. Salvaged timbers from the medieval church were used to create the sculpture. In this work, the resurrection is interpreted as Christ rising triumphantly from the flames. Spirals of gold curling round the figure, represent fire but also provide a vivid imagery which is often used in this context to symbolise the power of the Holy Spirit.

The sculpture was the gift of Fred and Mavis Barber, Canon Bryan Barrowdale, Mick and Gill Kendrick and Dr David and Gill Sibley.

medieval niche beside rood screen, south wall
112cm x 36cm
wood, copper, gold leaf
acquired 1991

This sculpture depicts an older Christ Child seated on his mother's knee. The hands are very eloquent in this work. Mary's right hand protects and holds him, whilst her left releases him, giving her son to the world. Mary's face is peaceful and her eyes are closed as she inwardly contemplates what is to come. Beyond the sense of loss that all parents feel as their children grow up and leave them, there is more: there is the sense of inevitability and resignation. Yet Mary is not weak and tearful; she is strong and self-controlled. The child's hands are held open in a simple gesture of invitation and acceptance, and his intently gazing eyes give his face a frank expression which conveys a look of both innocence and wisdom. The complexity of the sculpture provides the onlooker with much to contemplate.

This work was created from timbers taken from a ruined stable at Ossington Hall, Nottinghamshire and was a combined gift from friends of cancer sufferers in Lambley Parish.

*placed in sanctuary during
Christmas season
dimensions of stable
122 x 103 x 66cm
mixed media, acquired 1994*

This nativity scene consists of the Holy Family, three shepherds and three wise men enclosed within a stable, with the ox and ass peering over the stable wall. With its elaborate canopy resembling an exotic baldachino, it has a more oriental quality than other cribs by Peter Ball. The scene is full of rich detail, set off by a flamboyant use of colour and design.

The work was purchased through private gifts and a donation from "Art in Churches".

CRIB

placed in front of nave altar during Season
dimensions of stall 76 x 183cm
mixed media
acquired 1994

In "glorious technicolour", this is a traditional representation of the Christmas story. The Nativity scene is placed in a rustic setting complete with ox and ass peering over the stable walls. The broken-down walls and pillars leave the group open to the night sky so that the Holy Family shines out with a brilliance that contrasts with the humble surroundings. Mary wears a star studded gown, and her golden face radiates love, as she kneels before her newborn Child, wrapped in swaddling bands, lying peacefully asleep. The three shepherds, leaning on their crooks, dressed in simple rough cloaks, bring two delightful fleecy lambs. In splendid crowns and garments decorated with exotic and luxurious designs, the three wise men kneel to offer their gifts. The Christmas star surmounts this charming tableau.

"Like stepping into a Christmas card"

north wall of crossing
137 x 46cm
old oak, copper, gold leaf, brass
acquired 1989

An anonymous benefactor was moved by this tender image of the Madonna and Child, and felt it belonged in this cathedral with which his family has strong connections. The gift was made in recognition of the cathedral's role as a spiritual centre of the diocese and in tribute to the memory of Anthony Thorold, the Bishop of Rochester and later of Winchester. This bishop had the vision that the cathedral, which had fallen into decay since it was a medieval priory, should be restored to serve the population of South London.

This rich and graceful sculpture is a handsome addition to the many elaborate monuments to be found in the cathedral. Mary is shown as Queen of Heaven wearing a crown. Her figure is constructed from an oak beam removed from a derelict stable building. The wood has been braced with an iron bar held in place with sturdy bolts down its length and yet the result is beautifully poised. The figures are heavily stylised but this is no stiff portrait, for although Mary is regal she is not aloof - here is a warm and touching image of Motherhood. Her baby, wrapped in swaddling bands, is not physically attached to the rest of the sculpture - he can literally be snatched from Mary's enfolding arms! This reminds us of how dependent the baby is on the love and protection of his mother and how lost and defenceless he would be without her.

suspended before east window
155 x 122cm
wood, copper, gold leaf
acquired 1995

This elegant and powerful sculpture represents the resurrected Christ in full glory. The stylisation of the halo, the braided hair and drapery ornamented by a crudely polished rock crystal are reminiscent of early Italian images of Christ, such as the Christo Majestad taken from a monastery in Lucca, now in the Museo Maré, Barcelona.

Peter Ball has created an elaborate and majestic work for this richly ornamented setting. The figure shines out against the luminous backcloth of the stained glass west window - the whole effect is stunning.

SAINT, PILGRIM, SINNER
MAXIMUM HEIGHT 110cm

high altar
35 x 28cm
mixed media
acquired 1992

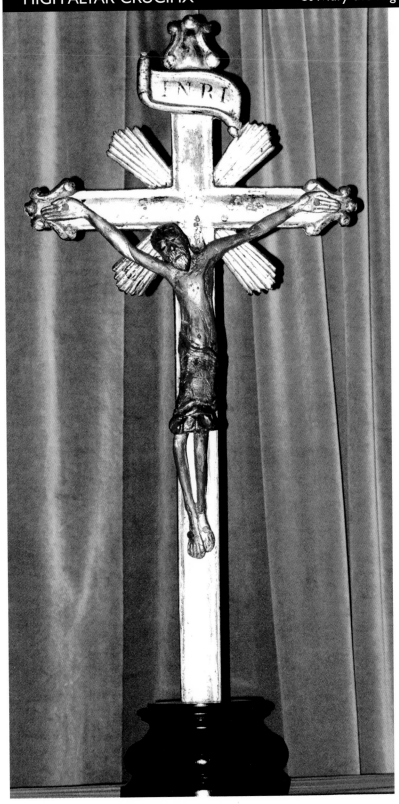

On the High Altar, this exquisite little crucifix is the smallest figure of Christ that Peter Ball has made for public display. The eighteenth century cross, found in a junk-shop, has acquired an attractive patina of age and wear. On the body of Christ, here and there the red ground shows through the gilding, as if the sculpture bleeds, like some miraculous medieval icon. Perhaps the sculpture needs to be placed in a small chapel, as it repays close attention and might be a focal point for private prayer, although its use on the high altar is equally poignant, to serve as a powerful image during Holy Communion.

north transept
203 x 152cm
wood, copper, gold leaf
acquired 1992

Here we see one of the most beautiful and lyrical contemporary images of Christ. The elaborate robes are decorated with discs of light swirling about a body which seems to be swaying gently, as if floating on air. The rhythm of these shapes, the attitude of the head - tilted slightly - and the dangling feet, suggest a sort of spiritual trance. Christ's eyes are closed, not in sleep, but in divine concentration. Here is a Christ who is listening intently, absorbed, patient and compassionate.

behind pulpit
110 x 95cm
wood, copper, semi-precious stones, gold leaf
acquired 1992

The simple stylised form of this image of the Risen Christ, is reminiscent of the type of work created by the Arts and Craft Movement in its symmetry and use of surface decoration. The beaten metal panels and central disc set with semi-precious stones are typical of the careful attention to detailed workmanship that was cultivated by that group of artists. The interior of the church has been scraped of its plaster; this radiant figure provides warmth and richness against the cool bare stone.

An adjoining plaque reads:

The above sculpture of the Risen Christ in Glory by Peter Ball is given in loving memory of Ethel Scrugham born 29 September 1913, died 9 February 1991.

The sculpture was donated by her husband, Reg Scrugham.

east end of nave
120 x 128cm
drift wood, copper, gold leaf
acquired 1988

Although it is constructed from driftwood left in its natural rough shape, the pieces have been so brought together, with the addition of stylised head, hands and legs, to create a very sophisticated and elegant Christus. The figure is beautifully poised, hanging on the east end of the nave beneath a stone gallery known as the Jube, originally constructed as a platform from which the gospel should be sung during liturgy, but now supporting the organ case. The nave, completed in 1991, provides a very light and airy space. Its plain pillars and white walls create a calm and uncluttered setting adding to the air of serenity of this Christus.

It was the generous gift of a young couple, who saw it at an exhibition in the cathedral, and donated it anonymously to the cathedral.

niches in east wall of sanctuary
all approximately 85cm in height
mixed media
acquired between 1994 - 1998

The collection of four figures in the niches at the east end of the sanctuary was created in two stages. The first to be acquired was that of St Thomas of Canterbury, which was commissioned by Colin James, the Bishop of Winchester (Portsmouth's 'mother diocese') in 1994, to mark the completion of the cathedral.

The remaining figures were purchased in 1998 with a legacy from Richard George Corbet Corbet-Milward, an Honorary Canon of the Cathedral. The figures represent important saints and bishops in the continuity of Christian worship.

Top left: St Augustine, first Archbishop of Canterbury, sent by Pope Gregory the Great to re-evangelise the English Church, represents the Roman element of early English Christianity.

Top right: St Thomas, Bishop and martyr and the patron saint of Portsmouth Cathedral; the sword through his mitre signifies his murder in Canterbury Cathedral.

Bottom left: Bishop Lancelot Andrewes, a distinguished Bishop of Winchester from 1619 to 1626, represents the post-reformation element of Christianity. In his day the diocese of Winchester included Portsmouth.

Bottom right: St Columba, Abbot of Iona, who brought Christianity to Scotland, represents the Celtic element of Christian conversion.

CRUCIFIX

St Mary's Church, Preston-on-Stour, Warwickshire

north wall of nave
140 x 120cm
wood and copper
acquired in 1978

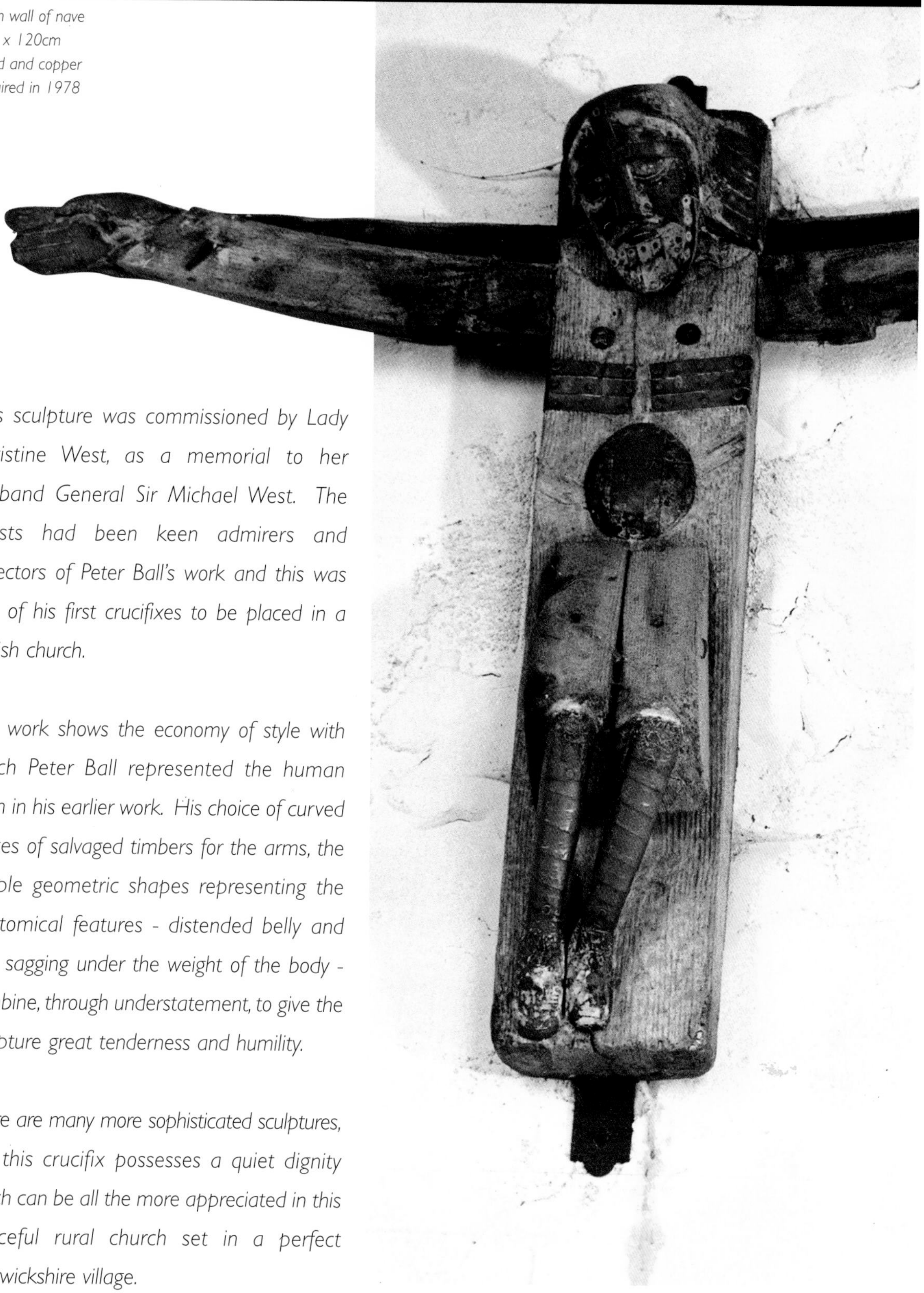

This sculpture was commissioned by Lady Christine West, as a memorial to her husband General Sir Michael West. The Wests had been keen admirers and collectors of Peter Ball's work and this was one of his first crucifixes to be placed in a parish church.

The work shows the economy of style with which Peter Ball represented the human form in his earlier work. His choice of curved pieces of salvaged timbers for the arms, the simple geometric shapes representing the anatomical features - distended belly and legs sagging under the weight of the body - combine, through understatement, to give the sculpture great tenderness and humility.

There are many more sophisticated sculptures, but this crucifix possesses a quiet dignity which can be all the more appreciated in this peaceful rural church set in a perfect Warwickshire village.

south transept
60 x 30 x 10cm
wood, copper, gold leaf
acquired 1993

This sculpture in bas-relief is made to fit within the dimensions of a sealed doorway in the south transept. It perfectly mirrors the proportions of the Romanesque arch. Its small size does not diminish the power of the image: that of a grieving mother cradling her dead son. Rather, there is a sense of intimacy which intensifies the message that the work conveys.

This piece was commissioned as a memorial to Pamela Irvine, and donated by her husband Murray Irvine, Provost of Southwell Minster until 1991.

chapel of Christ the Light of the World,
east end
100 x 30 cm
wood, copper, gold leaf
acquired 1990

Standing with outstretched arms, this gentle figure of Christ is small and approachable, as befits a chapel set aside for private prayer.

In an age when church-going is less frequent, many people find it difficult to come to terms with their spirituality and feel awkward about praying openly, so to stop and light a candle provides an "excuse" to make a brief pause - enough time to say an inward prayer. This work was commissioned as the focal point for the candle chapel, and was purchased by the Cathedral Council.

Airmen's Chapel
170 x 30cm
wood, pewter
acquired 1997, but on loan since 1994

Christ is presented here with his hands bound, his eyes closed and his head bowed in resignation, a "Man of Sorrows, and acquainted with grief".

This powerful and moving work was given to the cathedral by an anonymous donor. It features in a series of activities called "Time Travelling" which bring exciting new experiences to school children. For many, this is their first visit to a church let alone a powerful and awe-inspiring building such as a cathedral. Pupils are encouraged to touch the sculpture and describe their emotions. Children invariably find the sculpture accessible and can readily relate to this life-sized figure in a way that overcomes many barriers. Touching and drawing helps the children to understand their inner feelings without being hampered by the self-conscious difficulties of expressing themselves in words.

"The Peter Ball sculpture gave you feelings you just can't describe..."

thoughts of a young Time Traveller.

suspended above crossing arch
270 x 240cm
wood, copper, gold leaf
acquired 1987

Southwell's handsome and well-loved Christus hangs triumphantly above the crossing arch, reigning supreme. This is one of the best placed sculptures of Christ, commanding the entire nave of the Minster with its dramatic Norman arches. It is a testimony to the power of the sculpture that its splendour is able to reverberate through this great space. The modelling of Christ's robes echoes the cabling boldly carved into the crossing arches and the richness of the copper and gold reflects warm tones in the local Mansfield sandstone.

This work was purchased from a donation given in memory of Mabel Lockwood, by her son.

"I liked the simplicity and its richness. The surface is so interesting with its brass and copper overlay, particularly the highlights on the feet, as if generations of pilgrims had kissed them..."

Jane Garnett, Hilton Hall, Cambridgeshire.

school chapel
103 x 26 x 30cm
old oak, copper, gold leaf
acquired 1998

The style of this work echoes certain French Romanesque Madonnas. It compares very closely with a sculpture to be found in Notre-Dame d'Orcival, Puy-de-Dôme, France, called the Vierge d'Orcival. The wooden icon dates from around the 12th century, but it was clad much later, in 1631, with silver-plated copper, hammered over the robes with the nails following the lines of the drapery. This is analogous to the evolution of Peter Ball's work, where the timber is often much more ancient than the other materials, which have known a previous existence of their own. Through these mixed media, distant and powerful spirits are evoked.

The Christ child is shown at about the age of twelve, his eyes closed in contemplation; his left hand raised as if preaching and the right hand extended as if in anticipation of revealing the stigmata. Mary's eyes are downcast, closely and lovingly observing her son, whilst her hands prepare to let him depart from her care and protection. The intensity of the facial expressions is heightened by a covering of gold leaf which creates an ethereal quality.

Displayed in the north aisle during the Christmas season, the crib consists of nine free-standing figures which are place in front of a shelter with the ox and ass looking on. A traditional nativity scene has been created with Mary, Joseph, three kneeling wise men and three shepherds. The infant Jesus in swaddling bands is lying in a simple dish-shaped manger. The figures are covered in vibrant surface decoration, reminiscent of illuminated medieval manuscripts.

accessible in Christmas season
height of tallest figure 81cm
height of shelter 142cm
mixed media
acquired 1991

Lady Chapel
137 x 76cm
oak, copper, gold leaf
acquired 1990

This is one of the few Pietas to be seen in churches in the British Isles. It is a work of remarkable restraint and dignity.

The sculpture shows Mary holding the crucified Christ. Her knees are spread to bear the weight of her dead Son's body; one hand supports his neck whilst the other hand is held, palm outstretched as if in offering. Her robes fall over his limp body and her face is a mask of sorrow. But overlying the pain and sadness is an almost palpable tenderness. This sculpture is a very moving image of bereavement. Several people have expressed their feelings by writing poems after having experienced strong emotions in the presence of the sculpture.

The local Roman Catholic community raised the funds to acquire this piece for the Lady Chapel.

wall of north transept
168 x 168cm
wood, copper, gold leaf
acquired 1990

This risen Christ wears a splendid heavenly robe patterned with cosmic designs of spiraling galaxies and flashes of fiery comets and shooting stars. There is a wonderful tension between this dynamic surface and the repose of the figure.

The sculpture was first seen by Mrs Pat Broughall, during a temporary exhibition. It had been hung on the wall of the north transept, which has now come to be its final location. The sculpture worked so well in these surroundings that Mrs Broughall was moved to make a gift of it to the Cathedral. It is one of Peter Ball's most beautiful images of the risen Christ, with his arms outstretched - as in his crucifixion - but then again it seems as if he is inviting an embrace. The gesture is at once resigned and exultant. The angles of the head and feet are especially expressive of a body that is broken, but about the work there is an aura of grace. It was certainly an inspired act to place the work in this magnificent setting. It is a memorable experience to stand in this vast empty transept with sunlight streaming in through an expanse of window, and look up at this dazzling image of Christ.

St John the Evangelist and Fishermen Apostles' Chapel (Silkstede Chapel)
altar - 120cm cube; saints - height 130cm
wood, copper, pewter, brass, gold leaf
acquired 1996

The chapel had been used for non-liturgical purposes for many generations and needed an altar and other liturgical provisions. Izaac Walton, Father of English anglers is buried here and this connection became the theme for the embellishment.

Peter Ball has created the sanctuary furniture comprising an altar table and two free standing candle-holders in the form of the Apostles Simon and Peter. The altar table is megalithic in proportions being hewn from a single block of oak; the surface decoration captures the freedom of freshwater fish darting through a swirling stream. Not only is the spiral evocative of running water as it eddies and gurgles on its way downstream, but it is also makes reference to the eternal spiral, an ancient symbol of the progress of the soul towards eternal life. The work is thus full of vitality, and like a rippling stream, it engenders a sense of peace and contemplation.

The rhythm and energy of Peter Ball's work is beautifully complemented by the oak seating made by Alison Crowther.

suspended above altar table
150 x 200cm
wood, copper, gold leaf
acquired 1991

An elegant and slender Christus which soars high above the nave, is framed within the chancel arch, imitating the graceful proportions of the gothic architecture.

Here is a gently bidding image of Christ, who appears to be presiding over the altar table, with his arms outstretched to receive the prayers of the congregation below.

This sculpture was donated by the Reverend Anelay in memory of his wife Mrs Jean Anelay who died in 1988.

COLOURED MADONNA AND CHILD

110 x 35cm ARTIST'S COLLECTION

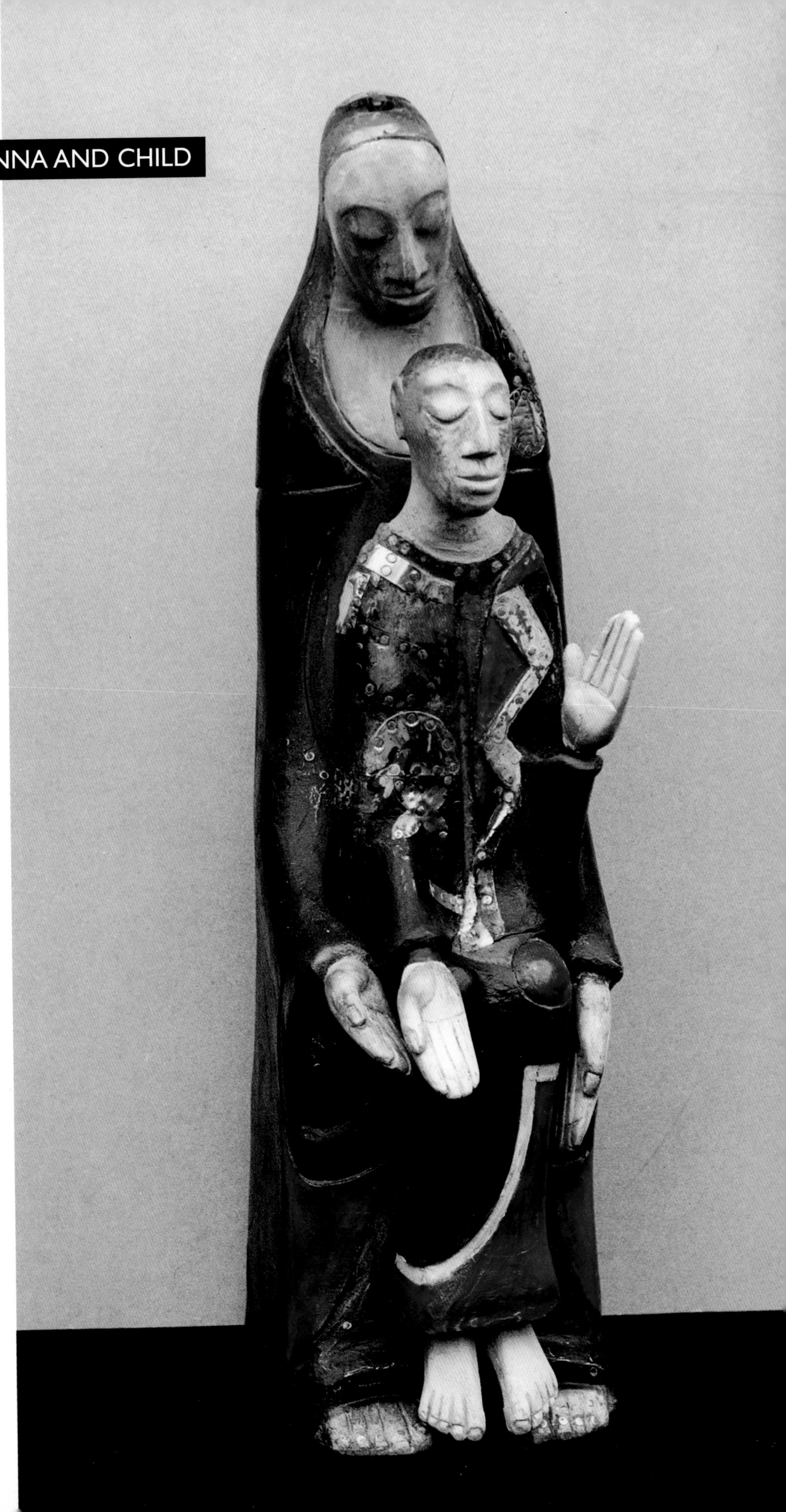

FOOTNOTES

1   Information about the statues in Westminster Cathedral taken from the article by Father Tim Dean and Patrick Rogers in *Oremus*, the Monthly Bulletin of Westminster Cathedral, May 1998, pp. 2-3.

2   cf. *The Work of Jean Dubuffet,* Peter Selz, Museum of Modern Art, New York 1962, p.102

3   A plaster mould for the molten plastic had to be made from an initial clay model.

4   These Catalan crucifixes were known as 'Majestads'. cf. *The Villein's Bible,* Brian Young, Barrie and Jenkins, London 1990, pl.V, VI and p.100

ACKNOWLEDGEMENTS

I would like to thank the following for their kind permission to obtain and publish photographs
for this book:

> The Dean and Chapter of Birmingham
>
> The Dean and Chapter of Southwark
>
> The Dean and Chapter of Southwell
>
> The Dean and Chapter of Portsmouth
>
> The Dean and Chapter of Winchester.

I am indebted to the many vicars, vergers, churchwardens and church administrators for their
kind assistance in allowing me access to the sculptures and supplying helpful information.

I am grateful to Nick Harding and Audrey Stocks, "Time Travelling!", Southwell Minster
and Jane Garnett for permission to use the quotations.

For their invaluable help and encouragement, I would like to thank:
The Reverend Canon Michael Austin, Colin Ball, The Reverend David Clarke, John Exton,
The Reverend Terry Hemmings, Penelope le Fanu Hughes, The Very Reverend David Leaning,
Roger Maris, Neil and Sally McDonnell, Valeria Taylor, The Reverend Canon Keith Walker
and The Very Reverend Michael Yorke.

A special thank you to Lyn Rickard for help with the text.

LIST OF PLATES

LIST OF MAJOR EXHIBITIONS

Majorie Parr Gallery 1967, 1970, 1972, 1974.

Gilbert Parr Gallery 1976, 1977, 1979, 1981.

Oxford Gallery, Oxford 1975.

Southwark Cathedral, London 1975.

Siau Gallery, Amsterdam, Holland 1976.

Zuoz, Switzerland 1977.

Burlington Fine Art Fair, R.A. London 1977.

International Art Fair, Basel, Germany Art 7 1976, Art 8 1977, Art 9 1978,

Art 10 1979, Art 11 1980, Art 12 1981, Art 13 1982, Art 14 1983.

Internationaler Kunstermarkt, Dusseldorf, Germany 1978.

New York, Chicago, Los Angeles 1980.

Steltman Gallery, Amsterdam, Holland 1981.

The Old School Gallery, Bleddfa Centre for Caring and the Arts, Wales 1983, 1987.

Alwin Gallery, London 1986.

McMurtrey Gallery, Houston, Texas, U.S.A. 1985, 1986.

Gilbert Gallery, Dorchester 1995.

Galerie Husstege, 's-Hertogenbosch, Holland 1988, 1989 -1990, 1995,1997-1998.

Southwell Minster, 1999.

BIBLIOGRAPHY

"Peter Eugene Ball. The Feel and Fabric of his Native Land." Paper; Max Wykes-Joyce.

"The Image of Life." Edward Robinson and Brenda Lealman (CEM)

"A Kind of Madness -The Sculptures of Peter Eugene Ball ." Inga Gilbert (Speedwell Books)

"Images or Idols? -the place of sacred art in churches today." Keith Walker (CPN)

"Images of Christ -Religious Iconography in Twentieth Century British Art" James Huntington-Whiteley (St Matthew's Centenary Art Committee, Henry Moore Foundation & Jerusalem Trust)

"Humour in Art" Nicholas Roukes (Davis Publications, Inc.)

INDEX OF WORKS

INDEX OF WORKS

The work of Peter Eugene Ball is to be found in private collections worldwide, in sculptures depicting all manner of men and women, beasts and chimeras, and a pantheon of gods.